How to Sell By Independent Sales Agents

A Step by Step Guide to Working With an Independent Sales Representative

I0463018

By Meir Liraz

Published by BizMove
www.bizmove.com

Table of Contents

MEIR LIRAZ

1. Cost and Control

The independent sales agent (also called 'sales representative')may be the answer for owner-managers who have problems with selling. In some cases, the problem may be that there are not enough prospects to justify putting a full-time sales force on the factory's payroll. In other cases, because of heavy schedules, the sales staff may be missing opportunities to cultivate new accounts.

This guide provides guidelines that should help the owner-manager of a small company to determine whether or not a sales agent is needed. Pointers are also given on how to choose an agent and how to work profitably with him or her.

If selling your product requires a salesman's or saleswoman's call, using an agent may be more efficient than having sales personnel on your payroll. Which is better depends on your situation.

Selling for others is the business of independent sales agents. They make their money by representing several clients on a commission basis. They solicit orders for clients in territories upon which they have agreed. Some agents have employees who help them cover a wide area.

The manufacturers, as a rule, ship and bill the customer directly. They set prices, terms, and other conditions of sale.

Sales agents go by various names. A few examples are manufacturer's agent, manufacturer's representative and "reps." The labels vary according to industry. Also, the marketing functions which agents perform vary from one industry to another.

Whether it is better to use your own sales force (direct selling) or a sales agent depends mainly on cost and control. Which method is more economical for you? Which method gives you the control of your, marketing that you need?

When you add sales personnel, what do they cost? In considering this cost, you should include items such as the paperwork necessary to keep them on the road; fringe benefits, such as vacations, hospital and other insurance, which you provide.

On control, the question is: What degree of control do you need to achieve your sales objectives? When an agent represents you, the agent controls the approach to customers. In effect, they are your agent's customers rather than yours.

In many cases, such a relationship may be as good as, or better than, using your own sales force. For example, if your products are attractive to distributors and retailers, it may make little or no difference whether they buy from a factory salesperson or an independent sales agent. When it makes no difference, the owner/manager who insists on maintaining a sales force for the sake of ego may be kidding himself or herself. You may be paying too great a price for the satisfaction of saying, "I have my own sales force. They are my employees."

On the other hand, when products require a special personal touch or service, the owner-manager may need to control the entire selling job. You may need to build an image by training and coaching your own technical sales staff rather than by offering your products through a manufacturer's agent who cannot usually be expected to do this type of work.

2. The Selling Job

In considering whether a direct sales staff or an independent agent is better, examine your company's selling job. the questions that follow are designed to help you think about the various aspects of that job.

Territories

In a given geographic area, does your company dominate, or does it lag way behind, competition? How near are you to your estimated potential sales volume?

What is your goal for that specific territory? If you had the best sales force money could buy, could your goal be achieved? If you could get only mediocre employees, what maximum dollar volume would you set for their quota?

What is your present dollar volume in the territory? What does it cost to bring in that volume? Based on these cost figures, what would your cost of sales be for achieving your ultimate sales quota?

How many dollars do you have to invest to build up a, specific territory? Does this investment (for salaries, traveling expenses, and supervisory expenses) run over a long enough time period to enable even a mediocre sales staff to reach your objectives?

Selling

Is your selling mostly service selling? (Service selling often requires technicians who can explain equipment and processes to middle management.) Is your selling nontechnical? (This type of selling does not require detailed knowledge of equipment and processes.)

What are the selling practices in your industry? Is there a good reason why the industry leans a particular way? Or is it just a custom which no one has thought of changing?

Market Penetration

How well do you know the market you are trying to penetrate? Do you know it well enough to guide your sales personnel? Or will you be relying on them because of your lack of knowledge of certain territories?

How often must the trade be seen? Can one employee handle all the calls? Or will several employees be needed because the area or number of accounts are too big for one person to cover regularly?

How quickly do you want to penetrate the market? (Someone with a knowledge of the field and personal contact with buyers will, of course, obtain this penetration more quickly than new employees.)

Cost

What is your cost for executive and clerical personnel to manage a direct sales staff in all your territories? (Break this cost down by territories.) What will it cost for executives and clerical people to manage an agent?

If you maintain a training program for your sales force, what does it cost? Does it pay off in increased sales?

3. Compare the Two

The statements that follow are designed to help you consider the advantages and disadvantages of direct sales staff and independent agents.

Training

Direct Sales. Finding and training new sales personnel can be time-consuming. Moreover, the cost can be high when employees quit shortly after they have received their training.

Sales Agents. With agents you can put them in the field quickly, and the training cost is nominal.

Type of Selling

Direct Sales. The sales person is, or becomes, a specialist in selling your line. It is easier to choose a person for a specific type of selling, such as service selling.

Sales Agents. They are specialists in selling only. They can seldom afford to offer service selling. Usually, they sell in a given territory and in a given product line and know their customers' needs. Often customers heed their advise because of the other items the agent sells them.

Experience

Direct Sales. You can hire a direct sales staff with any degree of experience. The degree depends on how much you are willing to spend and on what your situation calls for. The staff may not have the depth of knowledge of the territory and industry that you can draw upon.

Sales Agents. Normally, they will be experienced. Most agents are experienced professionals. Agents must have a depth knowledge of their territory and industry to exist, and it is there for your use.

Selling Time

Direct Sales. More time is devoted to selling your products.

Sales Agents. They devote only part of their time to your products because they handle a number of lines. But, in many cases, an agent has several people working so that you are buying their talents and time also.

Opening New Territories

Direct Sales. It often takes a direct sales staff a good deal of time to develop a following in a new territory. Even an experienced person needs time to accumulate detailed knowledge about a new territory. Investment can be high in starting a new territory or walking up an old one. Cash must be spent for the employees'' salaries and travel, sometimes for months, in order to build a profitable sales volume.

Sales Agents. Established agents offer a built-in following in given territories. They and their assistants have depth knowledge of the territory and the customers they serve. Moreover, an agent only gets paid on results.

Cost

Direct Sales. Employees' pay, if you want to hold them, has to be a living wage regardless of results. In an established territory, as sales go up, the results should more than pay for salaries and travel expenses. However, the cost of maintaining a direct sales staff may sometimes mean increasing their territory with diminishing penetration-loss of sales because of less frequent calls on customers.

Sales Agents. Their pay is a percent of sales. They pay their own travel expenses. In opening up new territories and maintaining sales coverage in territories with a limited yield, you pay for results. Coverage is concentrated in a given geographic area.

Paper Work

Direct Sales. Payroll and other clerical work is necessary to maintain direct sales staff.

Sales Agents. Only commission statements need be issued. The agents handle their own expenses, taxes, and have their own clerical staff.

Control

Direct Sales. You have complete control and direction of your own employees.

Sales Agents. The agent is free to operate according to the terms of your agreement with him or her.

To Summarize

Advantages of using a sales agent:

They can give you immediate entry into a territory. They can make regular calls on customers and prospects.

They can provide quality salesmanship.

Their cost is a predetermined selling expense a

percent of sales as their commission.

Disadvantages of using a sales agent:

Your control over their selling techniques is more limited than when you train and use your own employees.

On a large volume of sales, the selling expense may be excessive-greater than it would be with your own employees.

Agents' allegiance to your company and its products is not total because they serve other clients also. They have to have extra financial incentives to push your products.

If, and when, you cancel a contract, the agent may take many of your customers.

4. How to Select an Agent

If you decide that you need an independent sales agent in a specific territory, how do you select one who is right for your company? Every agent, no matter how good, is not right for every manufacturer. Selecting the one that can be an extension of your firm to the trade is not easy. To the customer, the agent is your company.

Here are some points to consider in matching an agent to your company's character and image.

What sort of selling skills are necessary for selling my products? Does the agent need technical knowledge and experience in addition to personal selling ability?

What marketing functions, if any, do I need in addition to selling?

Must the agent service my products as well as sell it? Do I need a one-man or one-woman agency or an organization? If the latter, how large an organization?

What is the agent's record of success in products and territories similar to mine?

How long has the agent been in business? What is the agent's reputation? How well can I trade on it?

Are the other lines carried by the agent compatible with mine? Will the agent's contacts for existing lines help gain entry for my line?

Is the trade the agent specializes is the one I want to reach?

Does the agent cover the geographic area I need covered and in what depth?

Do the character, personality, values, and integrity of our two organizations correspond?

Can the "reps", who are employees of the sales agent, sales-manage their own territories or will they need management and guidance from the agent? Or from me?

Is the agent the type that merely follows instructions? Or does the agent have a reputation for offering constructive suggestions? Which type do I need?

Is the "chemistry" right? Will we enjoy working together?

5. Sources of Agents

Once you know the kind of agent you are looking for, it becomes relatively easy to target in on the right one. You know what questions to ask the prospective agent. You know what qualities will satisfy your need. It is a matter of getting prospects from several sources. Those sources are:

Classified ads in trade papers nad on the Internet whose readership is geared toward the type of manufacturer's representative you seek.

Recommendations from customers and sales managers or owners of non-competing companies in your industry. Also, editors or salesmen and saleswomen from trade magazines can often offer recommendations.

You will probably come up with several choices. Agents are not hard to find. However, selecting the right one for you requires careful study on your part. Don't rush into a relationship. Getting the right partner is vital. Once the agent and manufacturer become associated, they are truly "married," so to speak. Their common goal is to get maximum sales from the territory.

6. Working With an Agent

A written contract is the start of harmonious relations with an agent. It should spell out what each of you is to do.

But don't stop after you've signed on an independent sales agent. Look for ways to get the most out of your relationship.

How do you motivate your agent to peak results? Unfortunately, here is where many manufacturers fail. They don't know how to work with a good agent. Often they blame the agent for their own shortcomings.

Actually, the formula for working harmoniously with an agent is fairly simple. Companies that work successfully with an independent sales agent accept the agent as a professional arm of their organization. Their owner-managers respect the talents of their agents.

Involve the independent sales agent in various phases of your marketing. For example, the agent may have constructive suggestions on packaging, sales promotion, and advertising. Many sales agents have strong ego drives and thrive on involvement.

When other clients lean heavily on the agent, you may have to fight to capture the agent's interest and get constructive advice. Hold your agent by making the agent part of your team.

Your communications must be clear and concise. The agent depends on you for information about your products, processes, and other matters that bear on selling for you.

The agent's interest, challenge, and profit - as does your profit-comes from making sales. Don't burden your agent with detail. Rather help cut through to the heart of what you expect your rep to accomplish sales.

MEIR LIRAZ

www.ingramcontent.com/pod-product-compliance
Lightning Source LLC
Chambersburg PA
CBHW070435180526
45158CB00017B/1290